KID HEROES
OF THE
ENVIRONMENT

The EarthWorks Group

Edited by Catherine Dee

Illustrations by Michele Montez

For Jesse. I hope you'll have a chance to be a hero some day.

THIS BOOK IS PRINTED ON RECYCLED PAPER.

Created and packaged by Javnarama
Designed by Javnarama
Cover design by Sharon Smith Design

ISBN 1-879-682-12-5
First Edition 10 9 8 7 6 5 4 3 2 1

We've provided a great deal of information about
practices and groups in our book. In most cases,
we've relied on the advice, recommendations, and research
by others whose judgments we consider accurate and
free from bias. However, we can't and don't guarantee
the results. This book offers you a start.
The responsibility for using it
ultimately rests with you.

Quantity discounts and special editions are available.
For information, please contact:
EarthWorks Press
1400 Shattuck Avenue, #25
Berkeley, CA 94709

ACKNOWLEDGMENTS

*Thanks to everyone who worked with us
to make this book possible including:*

- John Javna
- Catherine Dee
- Michele Montez
- Andy Sohn
- Fritz Springmeyer
- Lyn Speakman
- Lenna Lebovich
- Dayna Macy
- Melanie Foster
- John Dollison
- Megan Anderson
- Gordon Javna
- Joe Stubbs
- Craig Bristol
- Christine Shrader
- John Graham
- Tina Hobson
- Renew America
- Sharilyn Hovind
- David Eagle
- Jack Mingo
- Denise Silver
- Emma Lauriston
- James Sanchirico
- Brad Bunnin
- Sarah Dewey
- Chris Calwell
- Cindy Greene
- The heroes
- Household Hazardous Waste Project
- Ann Aronson
- Maura McKenna, Windstar
- Citizen's Clearinghouse for Hazardous Waste
- Environmental Action
- Amy Shapiro
- Chris Chandler
- Anne Rabe
- Dulcie de Montenac
- U.N. Environment Programme
- Karin Topping
- Rainforest Action Network
- Michele Roest
- Margery D. Rosen
- Hawley Truax
- Barbara Ruben
- Michael Williams
- Dave Cullen, EPA
- Jay Nitschke
- Graphic Detail
- Fran Javurek
- Sarah Dee
- Steve Purcell

CONTENTS

A NOTE FROM
THE AUTHORS

50 Simple Things Kids Can Do to Save the Earth was published in April, 1990. Since then, we've received thousands of letters from children all over the world. Some ask questions, some have suggestions, and many want to tell us what they're doing to help protect the environment. We love getting the letters; it's exciting to see that kids understand they have the power to make a difference.

Two years ago, we wrote about what kids *could* do to save our planet. Now we have a chance to share stories about what they're actually doing.

Why do we call them heroes? Because they're working to save the most important thing we have: Our Earth...our future.

If we really listen, we can learn a lot from these children. Their efforts have been an inspiration to us. We hope they'll inspire you, too.

—*John Javna,*
The EarthWorks Group

INTRODUCTION

W hen you're a kid, it can sometimes seem very hard to change other people's minds—even if it's to do good things, like protecting the environment.

It helps that many people now know about the dangers of pollution and the benefits of doing things like recycling and saving energy. But other people seem not to know—or not to care.

People who seem not to care are almost never *bad people*—they are just scared to get involved. They are afraid of being criticized for taking the lead or for doing something "different." Or maybe they are just a little lazy. Let's face it, it *is* easier to just hang out or watch television than to clean up a beach or write a letter to your senator!

At The Giraffe Project, we call people like these "Ostriches" because they seem to hide their heads in the sand and let others work on solving the problems.

The stories in this book are about people we call "Giraffes"—kids who are standing tall and "sticking their necks out" for the environment—kids who are *taking action*. As you read about them, I know you will be inspired.

When you put this book down, think of what YOU can do in your community to help. Then do it. I think you'll find that saving the Earth is exciting and fun!

—*John Graham,*
Executive Director, The Giraffe Project

KID POWER

"Sometimes we laugh at kids because we don't think they understand...but sometimes it's *us*, the adults, who don't understand. That becomes increasingly clear when we talk about the environment. We have to look to children as leaders."

—*Tina Hobson,*
Renew America

"Children manage to find the most creative and compelling ways to focus the attention of their parents and other adults on the importance of protecting our environment. Our children are the hope for the environment and the caretakers for our future."

—*Senator Al Gore,*
D-Tennessee

"People listen when children protest environmental problems...when kids started writing to Burger King, the company took notice and withdrew 35 million dollars worth of beef contracts from Central America."

—*Randy Hayes,*
Rainforest Action Network

"What children learn about the environment and what they do about it is the key to unlocking the mysteries to climate change, preserving our rainforests, and protecting ourselves from pollution."

—*William K. Reilly*
U.S. EPA

"I've heard parents complain that their kids are loud and argumentative about environmental issues. Sometimes they are—but that's what makes them Earth's best defenders. If the planet isn't worth raising a ruckus over, what is?"

—*Chris Calwell,*
Natural Resources
Defense Council

HEROES

AT
HOME

THE GIFT OF RECYCLING

Name: Mollie Clarke   **Age:** 17   **Grade:** 12
Town: Camden, South Carolina   **School:** Camden High
Goal: Convince her family and relatives to recycle

WHAT SHE DID

Summary

Mollie didn't know what to give her family members for Christmas. But the fact that they weren't recycling—even though she'd told them how it saves resources and helps cut pollution—gave her an idea.

Some relatives complained that it was too much trouble to get recycling bins that looked nice in their kitchens.

But Mollie was committed to recycling. So she came up with a novel way to solve the problem: Make recycling bins to give as gifts. "Then," she thought, "they won't have any excuses not to recycle."

Results

Mollie gave everyone handmade recycling bins, and they started recycling right away. "I encouraged them to help clean up our Earth and made it possible for them to do it," says Mollie. "Now I hope they'll spread their excitement and interest in recycling to others!"

HOW SHE DID IT

1. Mollie got some empty boxes from a liquor store (for free) and bought inexpensive wrapping paper to match her relatives' home decors.

2. She glued wrapping paper on the outside of each box.

3. She glued signs on each saying "Cans," "Newspaper," "Glass" or "Plastic."

4. She gave each of her relatives (her aunt and uncle, grand-parents, and immediate family) a set of 5 recycling bins.

5. Last, she attached a note that listed their town recycling center's address, and a few facts about each of the materials.

6. "I told them that if they wished, I would take the mater-ials to the center," says Mollie. "Luckily, they all were willing to take the stuff on their own."

YOU CAN BE A HERO

Give the gift of recycling. A few tips from Mollie:

• "Figure out what can be recycled locally before you make bins, so you can put the right labels on them."

• "Consider how much space will be needed to store each material. I have a large family and we drink a lot of milk, so I used a big box for plastic bottles. My grandad lives alone, so I gave him one large box with cardboard dividers."

• "Support each person's recycling efforts. A lot of people are real nice, but they don't take recycling seriously. Keep calling and saying 'I'm going to the recycling center, do you want me to take your stuff?'"

For more information on recycling:

• Get a free comic book called "Adventures of the Garbage Gremlin" for kids in grades 4-7. Write to: Office of Program Management/Support, U.S. EPA, OS-305, 401 M St. SW, Washington, D.C. 20460. Order # EPA/530-SW-90-024.

SAVING SEA TURTLES

Name: Christian Miller
Age: 13 **Grade:** 9
Town: Palm Beach, Florida
School: Palm Beach
Day School
Goal: Protect sea turtles,
keep turtle species from
disappearing

WHAT HE DID
Summary

Sea turtles are reptiles that live in the ocean; they only come to the beach to lay eggs. When baby turtles hatch, they crawl out of the nest (simply a hole in the sand), crawl to the ocean, and swim away.

However, there are several problems: Many baby turtles are eaten by dogs, crabs, or other animals...or they're stolen by people who sell the shells for jewelry, etc. And if turtle hatchlings don't make it out of the nest, they can die from the heat or the weight of eggshells that fall on top of them.

Christian grew up on a farm where he learned to love animals. So when he found a dead turtle on the beach behind his house when his family moved to Florida, he was shocked.

After finding more dead turtles, he decided he had to help them—even if it meant giving up many hours of his free time.

Results

In 1990, Christian single-handedly rescued over 3,500 baby

turtles. He's saved more than 12,000 over the past 6 years.

HOW HE DID IT

Christian was involved in a local beach cleanup program called CleanSweep. He told the organizer he was concerned about the turtles, and was referred to the Florida Department of Natural Resources. They put him in touch with other volunteers who spent a year teaching him how to rescue turtles so he could get a permit.

Armed with his permit, Christian set out to look for turtles in distress. Here's what he does on a typical day:

1. He wakes up about 7 a.m., before the sand gets hot, and walks on the beach for 2-3 hours.

2. He looks for tracks to the ocean made by baby turtles. He follows them to the nest, then marks the area with stakes so people won't step on it.

3. He digs the sand out of the hole until he finds eggs. "Usually, I find a hatched baby turtle that didn't escape with the others," he says. "I carry it to the water and let it swim away." Then he covers the eggs up again.

4. After he patrols the beach, he writes down the number of turtles rescued from each nest, the number that died before he could help them, and the number of hatched, unhatched, and fertilized eggs. He types this data into his computer at home.

5. At the end of each nesting season, he sends a copy of the data to the Department of Natural Resources. "They use it as part of their ongoing research on sea turtles," he says.

Achievements
• Christian won the 1990 Palm Beach Chamber of Commerce Board of Directors Special Award.

• "It's amazing how one thing leads to another," says Christian. "I've helped the sea turtles, and they've helped me. I've done two research projects for my school's science fair based on them." He wrote "The Effect of Human Assistance on the Sea Turtle Emergence Rate," and won first prize. In 1990, his project, "The Effect of Relocation on Sea Turtle Hatchlings' Emergence Rate," won first prize and got an honorable mention at the Florida Regional Science Fair.

YOU CAN BE A HERO
Learn more about protecting marine animals. Write to these groups:

• **Earth Island Institute,** 300 Broadway, Suite 28, San Francisco, CA 94133. If you send a self-addressed, stamped envelope, they'll send you coloring brochures on sea turtles and dolphins. Write "Attention sea turtle restoration and marine mammal projects" on the envelope.

• **The Center for Marine Conservation,** 1725 DeSales St. NW, Washington, D.C. 20036. (202) 429-5609. They'll send free fact sheets about sea turtles, dolphins, whales, etc. They also have a sea turtle coloring book for $1.00.

• **The Pacific Whale Foundation,** Kealia Beach Plaza, 101 N. Kihei Road, Kihei, Maui, HI 96753-8833. Write for info on "adopting" a whale.

GARDENING FOR THE EARTH

Name: Leigh Bradford
Age: 8 **Grade:** 6
Town: Wheaton, Maryland
School: Kemp Mill Elementary
Goal: Help reduce the use of pesticides

WHAT SHE DID

Summary

Pesticides and herbicides—poison chemicals used to kill bugs and weeds—have become a big problem for the Earth. They get in our water, hurt animals, and pollute the soil. They're not good for people, either.

Leigh showed that kids can do something to stop them; she grew vegetables in a pesticide- and herbicide-free (*organic*) garden. "I knew pesticides and herbicides poison birds, animals and water supplies and also get in the food," she says. "I didn't want to hurt the earth."

Then she teamed up with her grandfather and wrote a book about it so other kids could learn about organic gardening.

Results

Her organic garden was a success—and so was her book.
A Child's Organic Garden was published in 1989.

HOW SHE DID IT

1. Leigh told her grandfather about her idea. He agreed to give her 100 square feet of his garden space.

2. She learned about organic gardening—what tools to use, how to prepare soil, add natural fertilizer called "compost" to enrich it, and plant seeds.

3. Leigh planted seeds for corn, stringbeans, peas, tomatoes, potatoes, radishes, and other vegetables.

4. She gave up about 12 Saturdays and free time after school to tend the garden. About once a week, she watered it. She also pulled weeds.

5. After months of gardening, the vegetables were ripe. Some had aphids and other pests on them. "Sometimes before we picked them, we put nontoxic bug killer on them," Leigh says. The vegetables tasted delicious—"fresh and sweet."

YOU CAN BE A HERO

Be an organic gardener. For details:

• For a free fact sheet about pesticides, send a self-addressed, stamped envelope to Pesticide Watch, 1147 S. Robertson Blvd., Los Angeles, CA 90035. Specify "pesticide fact sheet."

• You can get Leigh's book for $10 from Earth Foods Associates, 11221 Markwood Dr., Wheaton, MD 20902.

• Another good book is *Kids Gardening: A Kid's Guide to Messing Around in the Dirt* by Kim and Kevin Raftery. It's available from Klutz Press, 2121 Staunton Ct., Palo Alto, CA 94306 (or check a bookstore).

WEEKEND WARRIORS

Names: Rebecca and Phillippa Herbert

Ages: 9 & 12   **Grades:** 4 & 7

Town: West Covina, California

Schools: Cameron Elementary & Edgewood Middle School

Goal: Save animals, help their community recycle

WHAT THEY DID
Summary

Rebecca and Phillippa Herbert were worried about the effects of pollution and garbage on animal life. "We saw a picture of a bird with plastic six pack rings caught on its beak," says Phillippa. "We felt sorry for animals and wanted to help them."

They decided to raise money and donate it to the National Wildlife Federation. But first they had to come up with a way to make the money.

They knew a lot of their neighbors had materials to recycle. "We thought, what if we start a recycling center in our yard?" says Rebecca. "That way, we could also save resources."

Results

Saturdays became known as "recycling day" in their neighborhood. According

Phillippa

to an article about Rebecca and Phillippa in the local *Tribune News*, "Their energy and vision has ignited a recycling revolution on the block." They've also made enough money to send donations of $50-$80 to the National Wildlife Federation.

Rebecca

HOW THEY DID IT

1. They asked their father to bring home some empty cardboard boxes.

2. They labeled the boxes with signs: "Glass," "Newspapers," etc.

3. They made flyers showing their address, the time the center would be open (9:30 a.m. to 12:00 noon), and what items they would accept.

4. Their father has a copy machine at his office, so they printed about 100 copies of the flyer.

5. "We took them to people's homes," says Rebecca. "We said, "Please help us recycle and save the Earth."

6. Every Saturday morning, they sat out in front with the boxes and waited for the neighbors to bring recyclables. "We had crayons, paper, and books to entertain ourselves," says Phillippa.

7. At the end of each month, the girls and their father

took the boxes full of materials to a recycling center.

YOU CAN BE A HERO

Start your own recycling center. Here are some tips:

• Find out where there's a local recycling center that will take your cans, bottles, and newspapers. Look in the yellow pages under "Recycling."

• Call and find out when the recycling center is open so you'll know when you can drop off (or have one of your parents drop off) the materials.

• Ask the people who work there how the materials should be prepared. For example: Do they want newspapers tied in bundles or left loose? Do you need to rinse out bottles?

• Make sure you let your neighbors know about your center! Make flyers saying what you're collecting, where you live, and when your center will be open. Give them to everybody on your block.

• For bins, get cardboard boxes from a supermarket or use garbage cans.

• To attract attention, make a big sign that says "Recycle Here" and put it next to the bins.

To get more information about recycling:

• "Rad Rick" will show you how to recycle in his coloring book, which is free from Mr. Rubbish, SWEEP, P.O. Box 666, Whitmore Lake, MI 48198.

A ROTTIN' PROJECT

Name: Matt Fischer
Age: 13 **Grade:** 9
Town: Charleston,
West Virginia
School: John Adams
Junior High School
Goal: Fight the garbage
crisis by composting yard
waste

WHAT HE DID
Summary

America faces a "garbage crisis"; we're running out of places to dump our trash. We have to throw less away...but how? One way is to compost at home—put organic materials like leaves and grass in a backyard bin instead of throwing them out— and let them *decompose* (rot) so they become part of the Earth again. Composting can cut the amount of garbage Americans throw out by 20%...but it takes an effort like Matt's.

Matt's family has a big yard, and each week after the lawn was mowed, he would wheel a 40-gallon trash can of freshly mowed grass and recently raked leaves to the curb for the trash collector. "What a waste," he thought.

When he told his parents yard waste shouldn't be thrown out, they agreed, but they didn't want to be bothered with composting. So Matt came up with a reason for doing it himself: He turned it into a science project on how quickly things can break down into compost.

Results

Matt estimates he kept 30-40 trash cans full of yard waste from being thrown away that year. His science project won first prize at his school and third in the county.

HOW HE DID IT

1. Matt's father bought wood for making a compost bin.

2. With his father's help, Matt nailed the bin together, leaving one side and the top open for adding materials.

3. He came up with a hypothesis for his science experiment: Grass and leaves would decay faster than any other material.

4. He put a box in his room with the "control" materials all mixed together: grass, leaves, newspaper, glossy newsprint ads, a brown paper bag and a magazine.

5. He put identical items in the compost bin, then covered them with grass and leaves.

6. Every day, he checked the temperature inside the compost pile to see if it was heating up (decaying material "cooks" itself). Sometimes it got as high as 120°.

7. He turned the pile (stirred it up) once a week, and added the new grass and leaves that had been raked up.

8. After about 9 months, he analyzed a sample of compost from the middle of the pile. His hypothesis was right; the grass and leaves had decayed the most. Newspaper came in second. The glossy newspaper inserts and magazine had hardly changed at all.

YOU CAN BE A HERO

For details on starting your own compost pile:
Write to the Berkeley Composting Center, 2530 San Pablo Avenue, Berkeley, CA 94702. Ask for their composting fact sheet. Include a self-addressed, stamped envelope.

OLIVER THE OTTER

Name: Aruna Chandrasekhar   **Age:** 9   **Grade:** 4

Town: Houston, Texas

School: Windsor Village Vanguard Elementary School

Goal: Inform kids about how oil spills affect animals and the environment

WHAT SHE DID

Summary

In April 1990, Aruna's 4th-grade

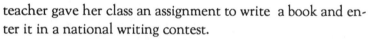

teacher gave her class an assignment to write a book and enter it in a national writing contest.

Aruna thought, "Here's an opportunity to help children learn about environmental disasters and the importance of preventing them."

She had read about the Exxon *Valdez* oil spill in *National Geographic* magazine and thought kids would want to know how sea creatures were affected by it. She decided to write about otters because "they've been hunted for their coats for many years, and they're almost extinct."

Results

She wrote and illustrated *Oliver and the Oil Spill,* a book about otters trapped in an oil spill off the Pacific Coast. In it, an otter named Oliver and his mother are rescued and have the oil cleaned off their fur. Although his mother dies, Oliver makes it back into the ocean.

The book won first place (out of 7,000 entries) in the 6-9 year-old category; Aruna won a scholarship for $5,000, and the book was published.

HOW SHE DID IT

1. She did some research to find out what happens to animals in an oil spill, how otters behave, and other facts.

2. She wrote the story, which turned out to be 24 pages. Then she went back and checked it to make sure she liked the way it sounded. It took 6 weeks to finish.

3. She drew pictures for the book.

4. One of her parents typed the story on sheets of white paper. She glued each sheet to a precut cardboard page, then hand-stitched the pages together.

5. She drew a picture for the book cover, added the title, and took it to be "laminated"—covered with clear plastic.

YOU CAN BE A HERO

Write a story about the environment. Even if you don't enter it in a contest, you can share it with friends and family.

• If you would like to have your class write books for the contest Aruna entered, find out if your teacher is interested. He or she can order a helpful guide called *Written and Illustrated By...*, from Landmark Editions, 1402 Kansas Ave., Kansas City, MO 64127. It's $17.95.

• Aruna's book is also available from Land- mark. Or ask for it at your local library.

HEROES

AT
SCHOOL

A POSITIVE DEMONSTRATION

Group: Mrs. Robin Ellenbecker's 5th-grade math class

Ages: 10-12   **Town:** Cheyenne, Wyoming

School: Anderson School   **Goal:** Make the community aware of a fast-food restaurant's "pro-environment" record

WHAT THEY DID

Summary

In November 1990, Mrs. Ellenbecker's class was learning how to plot points on graphs. One of the sample questions in their textbook used the term "endangered species." The students started talking about the endangered animals in rainforests, and someone said a certain fast-food restaurant bought beef raised on cleared rainforest land.

"We all got riled," says Mrs. Ellenbecker. They decided that fast food restaurants should do business in a way that doesn't harm the Earth. So for a class project, Mrs. Ellenbecker had them survey local fast food restaurants to find out if they were trying to reduce waste, avoid using styrofoam, etc., then plot the information on graphs.

After dividing into teams and visiting the restaurants, the kids determined that Little Caesar's Pizza had the best record of any restaurant in town. "Arby's and Little Caesar's had a run-off," says student Aaron Atwell, "but Little Caesar's had more paper products." To thank the restaurant, they held a "positive picket" demonstration out in front.

Results

Their demonstration was on the evening news; it raised the whole community's eco-awareness. "Even my dad started recycling," says Aaron. Best of all, according to student Lindsay Nicholls, they got many of the restaurants (second-place Arby's for one) to start doing things like recycling and switching from styrofoam to paper packaging.

HOW THEY DID IT

1. They picked 12 local restaurants. Then they divided into groups; each group was assigned to one restaurant.

2. At each restaurant, the kids asked the manager to answer questions like, "What are you doing to protect the environment?" and "Do you recycle?"

3. The kids also collected each restaurant's packaging materials—cups, clamshell boxes, utensils—to compare with the ones other fast food places used.

4. They glued the materials onto a chart next to a bar graph and plotted the information they'd gathered on the graph.

5. The kids compared graphs and evaluated the restaurants.

6. Someone suggested picketing the worst environmental offender, but student Becky Valdez says, "We didn't want to get sued." So they decided to demonstrate at the place that was doing the *best* job for the Earth.

7. They chose Little Caesar's and told the manager the good news. Then they marched in front of the restaurant for 45 minutes, chanting slogans like "Buy pizza here" and carrying signs saying "Little Caesar's Makes a Difference."

Achievements

They won a contest called "Earth Expo." Three kids received a free trip to the United Nations Earth Inauguration Ceremony in New York on World Environment Day, June 5.

But since the whole class had participated in the project, everyone wanted to attend. So to raise money, they had bake sales, car washes—even a trash "clean-a-thon." They raised enough for everyone to go.

YOU CAN BE A HERO

Take an environmental survey of restaurants in your area.

• Each time you eat at a place, save the packaging materials to compare with other restaurants' materials.

• Student Kyle Dix also suggests making a list of questions to ask the restaurant manager about its environmental record, with space for writing the answers.

• Aaron's advice: "Be thorough, otherwise your data could be wrong. I went to the restaurant I surveyed twice, and the manager got out the restaurant manuals and went through them to answer my questions."

• Compare the amounts of garbage each place produces, how much it recycles, etc. Then decide which restaurants are the best and let your family and friends know the winners.

SAY IT IN SPANISH

Name: Darlene Rodriguez

Age: 17   **Grade:** 12

Town: Miami Springs, Florida

School: Miami Springs Senior High School

Goal: Teach young Hispanic people about protecting the environment

WHAT SHE DID
Summary

As part of her work in a school club called English Speakers of Other Languages (ESOL), Darlene helps new Hispanic immigrants learn American customs and adapt to life here.

In 1989, it occurred to her that most Hispanic students in the group didn't know much about environmental issues and ways to address them. She figured that the 60% of the students in her county's public schools who are Hispanic probably don't have the same opportunity to recycle, conserve water, or do other environmentally responsible things.

Her solution: Write a brochure in Spanish to educate Hispanics about the environment and inspire them to get involved.

Results

After spending many hours researching and writing it, Darlene is finally getting her brochure produced. She expects many Hispanic families to become interested in saving the environment as a result. She says, "Kids at school will use it to educate their parents... who'll then take it to their work-places, friends, and churches."

HOW SHE DID IT

1. She chose a few key environmental issues that affected the local Miami Springs area, like protecting wetlands and preserving endangered species.

2. She found information about these topics at the Friends of the Everglades office, where she worked as a volunteer.

She also wrote to environ-mental or-ganizations for brochures. Four that ar-rived were printed in Span-ish, but all were *10-15 years old!*

3. She asked the people at Friends of the Everglades if they would pay the cost of producing the brochure, and they agreed.

4. She asked local ecology groups to allow her to list them on the back of the brochure as contacts for more infor-mation.

5. To find out what people wanted to know about the en-vironment, she enlisted members of the school's Science Honors Society to do informal neighborhood surveys. They showed people a list of environmental topics and asked, "Are any of these related to things you do?" and "What environmental issues are you interested in?"

6. Using the survey results and other information she had gathered, Darlene first wrote the brochure in English. (She wanted to make sure it was easy to understand and "so interesting that everybody who read it would want to take action.")

7. She translated it.

Other Projects

Darlene also thought of doing a public-service announcement on TV to educate immigrants about water conservation. With the help of her Science Honors Society advisor, she wrote a jingle called "Every Drop Counts," and the "eco-mercial" is now being produced.

Achievements

Darlene was named a "Giraffe"—someone who takes a risk and "sticks her neck out"—by the Giraffe Project.

YOU CAN BE A HERO

If you speak another language, use your skills to help spread the environmental message. A few ideas:

• Do a brochure like Darlene's. It doesn't have to be fancy; you can type it on an 8 1/2" by 11" sheet of paper, make copies, and hand them out at school or in your neighborhood.

• Offer to give a talk about the environment in Spanish (or some other language) about the environment at a youth center, school, etc.

If you don't speak a foreign language:

• Check with a foreign language radio station to see if they'll translate and broadcast a public-service announcement about the environment if you write it in English.

A GREEN YEARBOOK

Group: Trinity School's yearbook staff
Ages: 14-18   **Grades:** 9-12
Town: Longview, Texas
Goal: Educate other students about the environment and get them excited about saving it

WHAT THEY DID
Summary
The high school students on the yearbook staff at Trinity School thought kids in all grades should be more into environmental issues. Since they were producing the yearbook, they figured they could at least include a message about

saving the Earth. But then someone had a better idea: make environmentalism the theme of the whole yearbook.

So the staff came up with creative ways to include information about everything from recycling to water pollution "We wanted to communicate the issue so kids would get motivated," says 10th grader Jill Stephenson.

Results

According to yearbook advisor Ellen Herbert, "The yearbook turned kids on." It inspired students to become activists. For example, the Spanish classes made recycling posters in Spanish and kids in the elementary grades started a school recycling center. (The town didn't have one before.) Eventually, an environmental science class was even added.

HOW THEY DID IT

1. They put facts about the earth in each section of the yearbook and wrote articles about what students did during the year to recycle, save resources, etc.

2. They gave each topic a catchy title. For example: They used "Environmentally Sound" for the upper-school choir.

3. They used "green" graphics. The cover, for example, is a trash collage. "It has cardboard, aluminum foil, bubble pack...over a picture of a rainforest with a big recycling symbol in the center," says one yearbook staffer.

4. They used recycled paper. "Some people said it would look bad," says Mrs. Herbert, "but you can hardly tell it's recycled!"

YOU CAN BE A HERO

Turn a school publication into a forum for environmental news:
• One easy way to start: write a letter about the environment to the editor of the school newspaper.

- Join the staff of the school paper and see if you can write a column about eco-issues.
- To get up-to-date facts on the environment, Jill recommends reading the newspaper or *Garbage* magazine.
- If you want to use recycled paper for your school yearbook (or any publication), get several bids. Some companies add an extra charge for recycled stock.
- Jill says: "If you're motivated to get the word out, your enthusiasm will spread all over the school. The more stuff you think of that promotes the environment, the more excited the teachers and students get."

READING, WRITING & RECYCLING

Name: Brady Landon Mann   **Age:** 9   **Grade:** 3
Town: Vancouver, Washington
School: Eisenhower Elementary
Goal: Save paper and other resources by starting a school recycling program

WHAT HE DID
Summary

Brady had read about conservation and had started recycling at home. But at his school there was no recycling program. "I thought, man, at school, we're not doing anything," he says. "In my class, kids throw away about 8 pieces of paper a day, some with only a few marks on them." Brady didn't want to let things keep on going that way. He figured that even if he could get just his class recycling, it would help. So he wrote a

letter to the school principal about starting a recycling program.

Results

According to Brady, "All classes now recycle white and colored paper." Kids also started a volunteer recycling effort to recycle milk cartons at the cafeteria. (Volunteers get "teddy bucks"—play money they can trade for toys.)

HOW HE DID IT

1. Brady wrote a rough draft of the letter and typed it on his mother's computer. She helped him with the spelling.

2. It went like this: "Dear Mr. Maas:
I'm worried about our environment. If everybody helps save our Earth, we kids will have a better place to live in the future. We should recycle. This might take some work, but you could get students to help out. Once you get in the habit of recycling, it gets very easy, and you feel good about yourself."

3. The letter suggested that white paper and cafeteria items like tin cans, milk cartons, plastic jugs, and glass containers be recycled.

4. He gave it to the principal. In return, he got a thank you note back...and results. The school started recycling.

More Projects

Brady was so inspired by the success of the school recycling program that he thought of something else to do.

There used to be litter scattered around his apartment complex; maintenance people had been hired to clean it up. Brady thought kids living in the building could do a better job, so he asked the manager to hire the children instead. "Now we get $1 for every bag filled up," he says. "And we have a good-looking place!"

YOU CAN BE A HERO

If your school isn't recycling yet, you can suggest to the principal that he or she start a program.

• There's a booklet called "Recycling in School" available for $3.50 from the Pennsylvania Resources Council, P.O. Box 88, Media, PA 19063. It's written for teachers and kids 13 or older.

• Send for a free poster about recycling at school. It's called "Ride the Wave of the Future." You can put it up in your classroom or in the cafeteria to remind everyone to recycle. The address is: Office of Program Management and Support, OS-305, U.S. EPA, 401 M St., Washington, D.C. 20460.

PROJECT HOPE

Group: The HOPE Clinic   **Ages:** 9-11   **Grade:** 4
Town: North Myrtle Beach, South Carolina
Goal: Get parents, neighbors, and local businesspeople actively involved in protecting the Earth

WHAT THEY DID
Summary

In 1990, 4th-grade teacher Gerri Ferguson started a kids' environmental group called the HOPE (Healing Our Planet Earth) Clinic. The reason? She explains: "Earth Day made a big impact on me. And one person can do a lot, but you know, if you join a group at school or a community organization, your power is multiplied."

She and her students talked about environmental problems and ways to help. Then they resolved to do whatever they could by becoming "Earth doctors."

Results

The kids got everybody—friends, parents, relatives, neighbors—involved in keeping the planet healthy. For example, according to one HOPE doctor, Jessica Hoffman, "I come from an area that wasn't involved at all before. You had to go

way out of your way to recycle...Now there are more recycling centers and there's more awareness."

HOW THEY DID IT

Two of the group's projects:

A Campaign to Get the Community Recycling

1. They sent home "prescriptions" for a healthy Earth to their families, advising them to follow advice like "Recycle Cans" and "Reuse Paper."

2. Recycling was also prescribed for their school. The doctors made recycling bins out of trash cans and put them in the administrative office, teachers' lounge and classrooms.

3. They wrote a rap song about reusing and recycling and performed it for each class.

4. They wrote public service announcements reminding people to recycle and aired them on local radio stations.

5. They printed pamphlets about recycling and passed them out at PTA meetings and around town. As a result, more people learned about recycling.

6. They set up a program to collect old phone books for recycling. One student estimates that over 300 directories were recycled.

An Anti-Styrofoam Campaign

1. They wrote to their school district lunchroom manager and circulated petitions to the school board asking for a ban on Styrofoam. The district stopped using it.

2. They did research on restaurant chains that were using Styrofoam products.

3. They got at least 800 people to sign an "anti-Styrofoam" petition to send to the restaurants' headquarters.

4. They came up with the slogan, "Let's Make Styrofoam as Extinct as the Dinosaur," then made a "Styrosaurus" out of wood and nailed cafeteria cups and plates onto it.

5. They displayed the Styrosaurus in their booth at the high school "Neighborhood Awareness Night" and at the Earth Day '91 celebration

YOU CAN BE A HERO

Want to take on some big eco-projects? Start a group.

• Mrs. Ferguson recommends: "First find an interested teacher or some other adult leader to be your advisor."

• If you can't find an adult, you can still start your own club with friends or kids at school.

• Another idea: Join a club that already exists, then start a local chapter. There's a club called "Kids for Saving Earth;" if you write to them, they'll tell you how to get started. The address: Kids for Saving Earth, P.O. Box 47247, Plymouth, MN 55447-0247.

TREE'S COMPANY

Names: Patricia Arambula and Iris Ybarra

Ages: 15 and 16   **Grade:** 10   **Town:** San Antonio, Texas

School: South San Antonio High School

Goal: Plant trees to fight air pollution and beautify their school

WHAT THEY DID

Summary

In September 1990, school Science Club advisor Pete Alaniz suggested planting trees on campus as a project to help the environment. Two freshman girls, Patricia and Iris, thought

it was a great idea...But the other kids weren't into it. The seniors didn't consider digging holes fun.

However, that didn't curb the girls' enthusiasm. They took charge, and before long they had organized the club—including the seniors—into a formidable landscaping crew.

Results

They planted almost 100 trees, shrubs, and cacti during the school year. The program was so successful that teachers sent thank you letters and pitched in money to buy more trees—and the project is now a permanent Science Club activity.

HOW THEY DID IT

1. They read about trees. They found out, for example, that trees absorb carbon dioxide, the main gas that causes the "greenhouse effect." Trees also provide shade near buildings so less energy is needed for air-conditioning.

2. Club members made and handed out flyers, and put up posters about the project.

3. To raise money to buy trees, many kids held garage sales at home. The club also used money earned from a school recycling program, plus donations from teachers and students.

4. They did a little research to find out which species of trees grow naturally in the area, and which are drought-resistant.

5. They bought a variety of trees at a local nursery: live oaks, cedar elms, crepe myrtle bushes, and others.

6. After school and on weekends, they planted the trees around new buildings, in front of the school steps, and by the tennis courts.

7. Everybody pitched in by watering and putting fertilizer around the trees.

YOU CAN BE A HERO

For more information about tree planting, write to:

• **The Pennsylvania Resources Council,** P.O. Box 88, Media, PA 19063. They'll send a free pamphlet called "Planting Trees" if you include a self-addressed, stamped envelope.

• **The American Forestry Association,** 1516 P St. NW, Washington, D.C. 20005. Attn: Carolyn Hennrikus. Ask for their free action guide on global warming, how forests help stop it, and how to plant trees. It's written for high school students.

BEACH PARTY

Group: Students Tackle Ocean Plastic (STOP)

Ages: 10-12   **Grades:** 4-6

Town: Ocean City, Maryland

Goal: Clean up the beach, inform people about how plastic debris harms marine life

WHAT THEY DID

Summary

In 1987, a 4th-grade teacher named Sandra Hornung heard that large amounts of plastic debris were being found on beaches in many parts of the country. She wrote to environmental groups to get more information.

She and her students read the materials and learned that plastic garbage (for example, 6-pack rings, and shopping bags) can kill marine animals like turtles, pelicans and seagulls if the animals swallow it or get tangled in it. The children decided to do whatever they could to keep the animals out of danger. They came up with a plan to pick up plastic and other trash on the beach at nearby Assateague Island.

Results

The day of their beach cleanup, the group picked up about 100 large bags full of garbage.

Parents and friends were impressed that the kids had given up their free time...so many of them also volunteered to help. Now there's a STOP beach cleanup every year.

HOW THEY DID IT

1. They read the brochures about plastic and its effects on the environment.

2. They created a flyer filled with statistics, including information on how much garbage is thrown away in America each year, how many animals are found with plastic in their stomachs, etc.

3. They printed another flyer that listed the things people can do to help. For example: Write letters to congresspeople about the problem, and don't litter on the beach.

4. They passed out the flyers at a local boat show.

5. They presented a slide/tape show about plastic debris and ocean life to kids in the area.

6. They did public service announcements on TV, inviting everyone to the cleanup.

7. On cleanup day, children, teachers and parents (even grandparents) put on rubber gloves and picked up trash for 1 1/2 to 2 hours.

8. They worked in teams, with one person picking up trash and the other keeping a written tally of how many items were retrieved. STOP member Michelle Hornung says, "We found a lot of balloons, cigarette lighters, plastic bags."

9. Each team collected an average of 2 garbage bags full.

Sandra says, "We were flabbergasted, it doesn't look like there's that much trash!"

10. They left the bags on the beach for rangers to haul away in pickup trucks.

Accomplishments

As a result of the successful beach cleanups held over the past 3 years, some STOP members (and their parents) were asked by the Center for Marine Conservation to conduct a year-long "debris survey" for the organization.

YOU CAN BE A HERO

Keep trash off the beach. Some tips:

• Take a garbage bag with you next time you go to the beach and spend a few minutes collecting litter.

• Find out if there's a group beach cleanup planned in your town by calling city hall or a local environmental group.

• Nothing planned? Organize an event yourself. "You can just go with your family and friends in your neighborhood," says one STOP member.

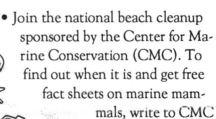

• Join the national beach cleanup sponsored by the Center for Marine Conservation (CMC). To find out when it is and get free fact sheets on marine mammals, write to CMC at 1725 DeSales St. NW, Washington, D.C. 20036.

FUND-RAISING FOR THE FOREST

Group: Erindale Secondary School Environmental Club
Ages: 16-18   **Town:** Mississauga, Ontario, Canada
Goal: Raise money to protect rainforests from destruction

WHAT THEY DID
Summary

Teacher Jon Kirby was concerned about issues like pollution, the garbage crisis and disappearing rainforests... and he wanted to share his concerns with students. "I knew there was a large body of young people out there who were just looking for an opportunity to get involved in something bigger than themselves," he says. So in 1989, he started an environmental action club.

In 1990, club members planned a two-week period in which they could teach students about the rainforests and raise money to "adopt" rainforest land. Each acre the school

"bought" for $25 would be protected by the World Wildlife Fund's "Guardians of the Amazon" program.

Club member Zoe Bandler says they picked the World Wildlife Fund program so they would know exactly where their money was going—"It was more tangible than just giving money to an environmental organization."

Their goal: Adopt 75 acres of rainforest (one acre for each homeroom).

Results

They raised about three times as much as their goal, and donated a total of $7,000 to adopt 280 acres. "We were surprised we were able to raise that much," says club member Ramee Singh. "It was satisfying to know that people did care. The campaign gave students something to believe in and work toward."

HOW THEY DID IT

1. The first week was dedicated to education, and the second to fund-raising. To help students learn about rain-forests before raising money, a quiz was passed out each day during homeroom. The environmental club members corrected the quizzes, and the homeroom with the most right answers that week won a $25 "head start" for the week of fund-raising.

2. Each homeroom was asked to come up with $25 to "buy" an acre, and was encouraged to be creative in doing it.

3. According to club member Matt Lloyd, one teacher took the initiative and said, "My class is going to do something totally wacko." She challenged other classes to raise as much money as hers.

4. Kids thought of all sorts of ideas (although some of the craziest weren't allowed). For example:

• There were singing telegrams. One participant explains: "For $2.00, students would go to a class and serenade the person of your choice with the song you requested."

• They set up a booth to sell "Jungle Juice" (Kool-Aid), hot dogs, and hamburgers made with meat that *didn't* come from the rainforests.

• Some students bought acres of rainforest for their families for Christmas.

5. Teachers got into the act. Some provided their own incentives for raising money. For example, the vice principals held a raffle, and the winners got to throw pies at them.

6. A teacher-student basketball game was held during last class one Friday. Ticket sales brought in almost $1,000.

YOU CAN BE A HERO
For more information about how you can save rainforests:

• **Rainforest Action Network,** 301 Broadway, Suite A, San Francisco, CA 94133. Has a free fact sheet for students about creative fund-raising, plus other materials.

• **The Children's Rainforest,** P.O. Box 936, Lewiston, ME 04240. Coordinates donations to a rainforest conservation group called the Monteverde Conservation League.

• For info on World Wildlife Fund's rainforest program: 90 Eglinton Ave. E, Ste 504, Toronto, ONT M4P-2Z7, Canada.

LOCAL

HEROES

PROTECTING A PARK

Names: Kate Crowther,
Sarah Crowther,
Laura Sheppard-Brick,
Ariana Wohl

Ages: 9-10 **Grade:** 5

Town: Northampton,
Massachusetts

School: Jackson St.
School

Goal: Protect trees in a
local park

WHAT THEY DID

Ariana

Summary

In 1989, the Northampton department of public works
decided to cut down 12 full-grown trees in Childs Park to
make a road wider and add parking spaces.

When Sarah and Kate heard the news, they told their
friends Ariana and Laura about it.

All of them were concerned. Ariana pointed out that trees
help keep our air clean. Sarah was concerned because animals
like squirrels and birds would lose their homes. She says, "It
was hard to imagine that one day there would be a park, and
the next day there would be parking spaces."

The girls agreed: They had to stop the project; they would
do whatever it took. Within days, they were staging a protest
in front of the park.

Results

The park was saved, and the street was left as it was. And, Laura says, "I think a lot of the kids in this town have become more environmentally conscious as a result."

HOW THEY DID IT

1. They considered their options. Sarah's mother suggested they picket—hold up signs at the park—and they liked the idea. They also decided to write letters to the mayor and start a petition.

2. They made signs saying, "Save our trees, save our animals!" and "If you care, please honk your horn!"

3. They asked their friends to help picket, but they didn't let adults participate. "We wanted it to be strictly a kids' event," says Ariana. They called their group Community Children to Save Our Park (CCSOP).

4. They picketed for 2 days. Sarah says, "People were very supportive: we got about 500 honks."

5. As a result of the picketing, the mayor came to Laura's house and met with the neighbors and protesters. Some people—like the engineer who did the plans for the wider street—opposed saving the park. He said, "An intersection is forever, a tree can always be planted again." But in the end, most people agreed with the kids.

YOU CAN BE A HERO

• "Don't be afraid to tell people what you think," says Laura. "One kid's father told us to wait until fall to picket. We said they were going to cut down the trees in two weeks, so we didn't want to take any chances."

• "Don't be afraid to tell the media what you're doing," says Laura. "I was scared to tell our local newspaper about our plans, because the article I'd read made it sound like the trees were already doomed. But the newspaper people aren't in charge. They just want news."

• How do you deal with the people who are against what you're doing? Laura says, "If they don't have much power, just ignore them. If they do, try to get someone more powerful on your side. In our case, it was the mayor."

Here are groups to contact for information on how to protect a park or a piece of open space—and the animals that live in it:

• **The Wilderness Society**, 900 17th St. NW, Washington, DC 20006. Free flyers about wildlife.

• **National Wildlife Federation,** 8925 Leesburg Pike, Vienna, VA 22184-0001. Has a free booklet for kids about protecting wildlife and other topics. It's called "You Can Do It;" ask for item #77003.

SAVE THE MANATEE

Name: Lyle Solla-Yates   **Age:** 10   **Grade:** 5
Town: Miami Shores, Florida   **School:** Cushman School
Goal: Protect manatees and other endangered species

WHAT HE DID
Summary
When Lyle was in first grade, his favorite animals were manatees, rare mammals also known as "sea cows." They live off the coast of Florida.

One day, Lyle read a report in the newspaper about a manatee that had been injured by a motorboat. It made him angry. "I really wanted to do something to help the manatees," he says. So in 1989, he started a group called "Pals of Wildlife" to raise money to help save them.

Results
His group raised hundreds of dollars and has donated the money to various environmental organizations. Lyle says, "We've gotten people to see they can change things. And we learned that helping the environment can be fun!"

HOW HE DID IT
1. He called his friends to tell them he was starting the group and when the first meeting would be. About 20 kids joined.

2. At the first meeting, they agreed to support efforts to protect endangered species like panthers and whales, too.

3. They thought of the name "Pals of Wildlife," and a motto: "When the animals die, we're dead meat."

4. They designed T-shirts with their name and motto. Each club member drew a small picture and wrote a slogan to go with it, like "Don't pollute." These were each printed in squares on the T-shirts.

5. To raise money, they sold the T-shirts. In addition, a club member asked a local pencil supplier to print "Pals of Wildlife" on pencils. Then the kids sold the pencils for 25¢ each.

6. They had fundraisers like an "Earthday Birthday" party, with tree planting, ecology-oriented arts and crafts, and games.

7. For the fund-raisers, each Pal's family handled one job, like bringing "Birthday" cake or coordinating tree planting.

8. They donated the money earned from the fund-raisers to the Children's Rainforest Project and Greenpeace.

YOU CAN BE A HERO

"Adopt" a manatee or another endangered animal. For info:

• **Save the Manatees,** Florida Audubon Society, 500 North Maitland Ave., Maitland, FL 32751. (800) 432-5646.

• **Humane Society,** 67 Salem Rd., East Chattam, CT 06423. Attn: Willow Soltow. They have a free "Kid's Guide to Saving the Earth and Its Animals" for students in grades 2-6.

THE TOXIC AVENGERS

Group: The Toxic Avengers   **Ages:** 12-21

Town: Brooklyn, New York

Goal: Shut down a hazardous waste storage facility in Williamsburg, a section of Brooklyn

WHAT THEY DID

Summary

The "Toxic Avengers" were born when Jose Morales, a science teacher at the local youth center, noticed that barrels of hazardous waste had been dumped in a nearby vacant lot. He and his students sent samples of the waste to a lab to see if it was toxic. They protested against the company that had dumped the barrels, and it stopped the dumping. As a result of this project, a group called the Citizens' Committee for New York decided to donate money so the Toxic Avengers could do more work.

Two Toxic Avengers plan their strategy

The students' next project: Get a hazardous waste storage facility out of their community. It was a challenging goal, since state officials were trying to *expand* the company that owned the storage facility so it could process *all* of New York State's hazardous waste.

But that didn't stop the Toxic Avengers—they launched a huge campaign to teach their neighborhood about the dangers of toxic waste.

Results

The Community Board voted in favor of closing down the facility, and a city councilmember came up with a resolution to prevent its expansion. Mr. Morales credits "the depth of community opposition" in the success.

The group members also learned how much power they have. Member Kathy Rivera says, "It really doesn't matter how old you are, how rich or poor, or what race you are—you can change things."

HOW THEY DID IT

1. They held week-ly planning meet-ings. They decided that "adultism"— Mr. Morales' term for the way adults tell kids what to do—would not be allowed.

2. They wrote a flyer about the toxic waste facility, copied it, and passed it out to

people in their area.

3. They asked people if they'd heard about the facility. "A lot of people didn't even know it existed—they were pretty upset," says Kathy.

4. They put on slide presentations for people who wanted to learn more.

5. They recruited people to protest. It wasn't easy because the facility is in a minority (Hispanic) neighborhood— "People are too poor, too busy working and worrying about their kids to protest," says Kathy.

6. They held a public meeting at an elementary school a block from the facility. About 200 people showed up.

7. They held 3 protest marches and rallies in front of the school. Politicians, religious leaders, and parents attended. Some held signs saying things like "No Cancer for Our Kids."

YOU CAN BE A HERO
Find out more about how to keep hazardous materials from damaging the earth.

• **The National Toxics Campaign,** 1168 Commonwealth Ave., 3rd Floor, Boston, MA 02134. Has fact sheets on hazardous waste, household toxics, etc.

• **Citizens' Clearinghouse for Hazardous Waste,** P.O. Box 6806, Falls Church, VA 22040. What's available: A kids' fact packet with info on toxic waste, stories about what kids are doing, and a resource guide that shows what you can do in your area. It's $3.00 (includes postage).

SAVING WETLANDS

Name: Bradley Roberts
Age: 16
Grade: 11
Town: Aynor, South Carolina
School: Aynor High School
Goal: Get people to write letters and make phone calls to save endangered wetlands

WHAT HE DID

Summary

Wetlands—areas like swamps and marshes—are very important to the environment. They're the home and breeding grounds for many valuable birds and animals, they help reduce flooding, and they fight water pollution.

Bradley found out from his science teacher that wetlands are being destroyed all over the U.S. to make space for houses, office buildings and other developments. Even in his own "backyard," local wetlands have recently been turned into golf courses.

Disappointed that "humans are more interested in short-term investments at the risk of our natural resources," Bradley started an activist group in his local Audubon Society chapter to speak up about preserving wetlands.

Results

He recruited about 35 people (mostly adults) from the chapter to protest wetlands destruction by writing and calling congresspeople, senators, and the President regularly. He says, "I helped people see how easy it was for them to do something. Just one letter a month can make a big difference in the area and in the country."

HOW HE DID IT

1. He joined the local Audubon Society chapter (his science teacher, the chapter president, told him about it).

2. He read a newsletter called *The Audubon Activist*, which has tips for contacting legislators about the wetlands (and includes information about other ecology issues).

3. He realized the chapter members cared about protecting wetlands, but weren't doing much to save them. "People didn't write letters; they thought sending checks to the Audubon Society was enough," he says.

4. At the next chapter meeting, he made a presentation on how to be an activist, using the information he'd learned from the *Audubon Activist* and *Audubon* magazine. He invited interested people to come to a training meeting.

5. At the meeting, he gave people tips on how to write letters and make calls that would have an impact.

6. People began writing and making calls on their own.

YOU CAN BE A HERO

Speak up about preserving wetlands and other natural areas.

• The National Wildlife Federation recommends: "Call government officials when you hear that a building project is planned for a park or other wild place. Your municipal supervisor, city or county planning office, or other local government office may be able to explain the situation."

• For a free copy of the *Audubon Activist*, write to Audubon Activist, 950 Third Ave., New York, NY 10022.

• To find out if there's an Audubon chapter near you, write Chapter Services, 950 Third Ave., New York, NY 10022.

A RECYCLING PROGRAM

Laura-Beth and the state resolution passed in her name

Name: Laura-Beth Moore

Age: 12   **Grade:** 7

Town: Houston, Texas

School: Seton Catholic Junior High

Goal: Start a curbside recycling program in her city

WHAT SHE DID
Summary

On Earth Day 1990, Laura-Beth's school held a day-long recycling event, accepting materials from students' homes. When she saw how many bags of materials were brought in, she thought, "Why doesn't the city pick up these items from people's houses?"

She checked into the situation and found that the local garbage company was already picking up materials from houses in the neighborhood next to hers on a trial basis. But nobody was getting curbside recycling started in other areas.

So Laura-Beth decided to start a neighborhood recycling

effort. "I thought it was a great goal, and that it would be real easy," she says.

It wasn't. It took a year and a half to get a recycling program started.

Results

The program is now a success. Every month, neighbors drop off about 3 tons of materials at a central location. Then, on the first Saturday of each month, neighborhood volunteers take them to a recycling plant. The money earned is used to buy trees and flowers to plant in their area.

HOW SHE DID IT

1. She wrote a petition asking the mayor to have the city collect recyclables from houses in her neighborhood. She took it door-to-door to neighbors and got about 50 people to sign it.

2. She sent the petition to the mayor, but got a letter back saying curbside recycling would cost too much.

3. As an alternative, she decided to set up volunteer neighborhood recycling. She hoped it would eventually turn into a curbside recycling program.

4. She asked the president of the local civic club what he thought of her idea. He supported it and appointed her to organize the program.

5. All summer, she made calls to find someone to donate recycling bins, a place to drop off recyclables, people to pick up the materials, and other essentials.

6. People were not very responsive. "I would call places, and they would say, 'You know, you're just a kid, why don't you have an adult call?'" she says. For a month, she tried to reach the school principal to ask if the school grounds could be used as a place to drop off materials; no one called back.

7. In October, she went to another civic club meeting and told everyone what still needed to be done. Two members of the state house representatives who were there, and at least 15 other people, volunteered to help.

8. A volunteer finally contacted the school principal, who agreed to allow people to drop off recyclables on campus.

9. The first recycling collection day was held. At least 100 people with cars showed up, and altogether, 4,000 pounds of newspaper, 900 pounds of glass, 300 pounds of aluminum, 400 pounds of tin, and 4 truckloads of plastic were collected.

Achievements
To honor Laura-Beth, the state house of representatives passed a resolution in her name.

YOU CAN BE A HERO
If you want to start a program in your neighborhood, the key is to get powerful people like the mayor and state representatives to support you. Advice from Laura-Beth:

• "Politicians can help a lot; it pays to ask for their help." To find out who your state representatives are, look in the "government" pages at the front of the telephone book.

• "When I called companies, I learned to ask for the highest person" (the person in charge).

• "Be persistent. Bug people until they finally listen to you. Call back about 5 times a day—they'll get the picture."

BAT MAN

Name: Hunter Allen

Age: 8   **Grade:** 2

Town: Huntington, Massachusetts

School: Murrayfield School

Goal: Find a new home for bats living in the attic of a renovated community building

WHAT HE DID

Summary

Hunter had read about bats in *Ranger Rick* magazine. He was fascinated by these night creatures, which frighten people but aren't actually dangerous at all. (In fact, they can eat hundreds of insect pests in one night.)

Then Hunter's mother told him about some bats in the attic of North Hall, a nearby community center that was being restored. (She had seen them while doing electrical wiring in the building.) The problem was, the building maintenance people wanted the bats to move out.

Hunter was concerned that the bats might be killed or have trouble finding a new place to live. Then he remembered that the article in *Ranger Rick* had included instructions for making "bat boxes." So he set out to make some.

Results

The bats have a new home on the side wall of North Hall. It's not clear if they've moved in yet because bats take at least a year to get settled in a new place—but they have a place to go if they need it.

HOW HE DID IT

1. He sent away for the instructions from *Ranger Rick* (see address below).

2. Since he was in Cub Scouts, and the project looked like it was going to take some work, he recruited a few other Cubs to help.

3. They asked a lumber company to donate wood. The store agreed and gave them "rough-cut," unfinished pine.

4. They cut the wood into pieces and made 5 boxes.

5. Hunter's mother brought a ladder and nailed the boxes up on the side of North Hall.

YOU CAN BE A HERO

Be a bat saver:

• For instructions on building a bat box, send $1.00 to: National Wildlife Federation, *Ranger Rick* magazine, 8925 Leesburg Pike, Vienna, VA 22184. Note: It's a good idea to get an adult to help you make the boxes.

• For information about bats, write to Bat Conservation International, P.O. Box 162603, Austin, TX 78716. They have a booklet for kids aged 3-10 for $2.50.

ECOLOGY CORNER

Name: Sarah Melton   **Age:** 14   **Grade:** 10
Town: Sweetwater, Tennessee
School: Sweetwater High School
Goal: Turn the library into an environmental education
center for kids

WHAT SHE DID
Summary
Sarah—a Girl Scout who often works with young children—
watched a TV show about the environment in 1990. She
found it inspiring, but felt it should have been directed to
even younger kids. "Let's teach *young* children how to
protect the Earth," she thought, "After all, they're the next
generation…If they learn about it now, they'll continue to
care as adults."

She looked for ways
to get the message to
kids and came up with
the idea of creating in-
formative posters for
the children's room of
her local library.

Results
The librarian put
Sarah's posters up in
an area she called the
"ecology corner."
 Kids—and their par-
ents—appreciated it so

much that the librarian kept it going...and even invited Sarah to speak to children about the environment.

Sarah says: "I've been amazed at the response. Best of all, kids come up and tell me I've definitely helped to get them interested in saving the Earth."

HOW SHE DID IT

1. Sarah read books, brochures, and anything else she could find about the environment.

2. She asked the librarian for space to put up two posters at the beginning of the 1990-91 school year. "She was more than happy to make room," says Sarah.

3. She made two posters for each month. "The first poster had facts about an environmental problem" she says. "The second gave helpful hints, such as reducing use of Styrofoam and using the kind made without CFCs."

4. She got creative: "I tried to make posters coincide with the seasons. At Christmas, I did a poster on ecologically safe gifts, like donations to ecology programs."

5. The library staff wrote about the ecology corner in its newsletter.

YOU CAN BE A HERO

Start an ecology corner at your public library.

• When? "Next time you go to the library," Sarah suggests, "talk to the librarian. He or she might give you permission to start right away."

• How do you get information for posters? Sarah suggests: "Check out kids' books on the environment. There are so many out right now, it's not hard to find information."

• Use your imagination; your ecology corner doesn't have be just posters. A display of environmental books and magazines is a way to get kids interested, too.

TESTING THE WATER

Name: Dan Shuman
Age: 16
Grade: 10
Town: Dover, Pennsylvania
Goal: Find out the effect of "acid rain" on fish and trees; call legislators' attention to the problem

WHAT HE DID

Summary

In 1989, Dan noticed that certain fish had started disappearing from local lakes and streams. "I started to see fewer bass and trout, especially during the winter," he says. "Plus, trees were starting to die off in our backyard. You could pick them out—they didn't have any leaves."

He grew worried that the cause of this was *acid rain*—rainwater or snow that has mixed with pollution in the air and has fallen back to Earth as polluted water. But he didn't have any proof.

Then Dan read a story in a fishing magazine about a program at Dickinson College that provides kits for testing water for the effects of acid rain. "Why not make testing local streams a Boy Scout project?" he thought.

Results

The Scouts were eager to help; in fact, there weren't enough testing kits for all the boys at first. They monitored 22 streams for a year, ultimately proving that acid rain was a problem in the area.

Unfortunately, legislators aren't taking action to deal with acid rain yet. Dan says, "I've written letters and discussed the issue. They all say they're going to do something." And he thinks they eventually will…thanks in part to the Scouts' work.

HOW HE DID IT

1. Dan asked the Scout Masters of local troops if some boys could help out in exchange for service hours; they agreed.

2. He went around to Scout troops and asked for volunteers, recruiting about 15 boys.

3. The next challenge: Raising money to buy testing kits ($20 each from the Dickinson College program).

4. Dan went to 3 sports clubs asking for donations. "They were very helpful and generous," he says. In fact, they donated over $400.

5. Each Scout used his kit to monitor a different stream and then sent the results to Dan, who in turn, sent all the data to Dickinson.

6. After a year of testing, the people at Dickinson analyzed the data and sent Dan a thick report documenting that the water was contaminated by acid rain.

7. Dan went back to the boys and the clubs and told them the findings. "Afterwards, they were really fanatical about it," he says. "They wanted to do something." Some of them wrote letters and called legislators as a result.

YOU CAN BE A HERO

*"Adopt" a stream or lake near your house. For more
information, contact these groups:*

• **The Adopt a Stream Foundation,** Box 5558, Everett,
WA 98206. Send a self-addressed, stamped envelope for
tips on how your teacher can get your class involved in
protecting a stream.

• **The Acid Rain Foundation,** 1410 Varsity Dr., Raleigh,
NC 27606. For $1.95, you can get the "Rain, Rain, Go
Away" coloring book about acid rain, for kids up to the 4th
grade.

• **The Izaac Walton League of America** has a "Save Our
Streams Kid's Packet" for $1.00. The address is 401 Wilson
Blvd., Level B, Arlington, VA 22209. (703) 528-1818.

• **Trout Unlimited,** 800 Follin Lane SE, Suite 250, Vienna,
VA 22180-4959. Free information on trout-related projects
for outdoors clubs.

TRAIL BLAZER

Name: Bryan Kaplan   **Age:** 13   **Grade:** 8
Town: Manlius, New York
School: Eagle Hill Middle School
Goal: Protect wilderness areas and animals living in them

WHAT HE DID
Summary

When Bryan was 8, he heard about a program called "Walk to Save the County" at school. Kids would sign people up to sponsor them for a 10-kilometer walk; the money was used to protect and maintain land in the area. "I just wanted to do my part for the environment," says Bryan. So he began participating in the walk every year.

He went to people's houses and asked them to sponsor him. It wasn't always easy: Some people were rude and slammed the door; dogs chased him; one time, a little girl kicked him. "But," he says, "it's not really a hassle if I think of how much money I'm bringing in for the Earth."

He's brought in plenty: He went from a $20 contribution his first year to $635 to $1,100 in 1989. In 1990, he set a goal of $1234.56, and in 1991 raised $1,600.

Results

Bryan has contributed over $4,000 to the program—a record for any individual. The people at Save the County were so appreciative that they named a trail (marked with a plaque) after him.

HOW HE DID IT

1. Each year when the contest was announced, he went door-to-door in his neighborhood asking for sponsors.

2. "Usually, people wanted to help right away," he says. They gave $5 to $10.

3. He did this on weekends, and on weekdays from the time he got home from school until about 8 p.m.

4. He went on the walk with the other participants.

5. He went back and collected money from the neighbors who hadn't paid beforehand.

Achievements

Bryan was named a "Giraffe," someone who "sticks his or her neck out" for the community, by the Giraffe Project.

YOU CAN BE A HERO

Help protect open space and wild animals. For info, contact:

• **Defenders of Wildlife,** 1244 19th St. NW, Washington, D.C. 20036. Free brochure for upper elementary and junior high school students on endangered species.

• **Project WILD,** P.O. Box 18060, Boulder, CO 80308. Has an activity sheet about wildlife habitats which teachers can use in class.

NATIONAL

HEROES

FIGHTING FOAM

Name: Tanja Vogt
Age: 17   **Grade:** 12
Town: West Milford, New Jersey
School: West Milford High School
Goal: Get the school cafeteria to use paper instead of Styrofoam trays

WHAT SHE DID

Summary

In 1988, Tanja had an assignment to write an essay about a local current event for her U.S. history class. While researching it, an article in the newspaper caught her eye: Apparently members of the West Milford School Board had voted to continue using Styrofoam trays in the cafeteria instead of paper ones. Why? Styrofoam trays were a nickel cheaper.

Tanja says, "I read that article real carefully. I asked myself, why would we use these things if they're harmful to the environment?"

She wrote her essay about the school board's

decision, then wrote a note to her teacher saying she thought students would pay extra for paper trays.

Her teacher got excited. "He said if we stood up for what we believed in, it could be like a quiet revolution," Tanja recalls. So the class started a "Stop Styro" campaign.

Results

They convinced the school board to switch from Styrofoam to paper...and eventually to reusable trays.

But that's not all. They got plenty of publicity and inspired kids at schools all over the U.S. to start their own anti-Styrofoam campaigns. Many people believe the "revolution" they sparked was a key factor in McDonald's decision to switch from Styrofoam to paper packaging.

HOW SHE DID IT

1. Tanja and her classmates researched the environmental problems caused by producing, using and throwing away Styrofoam.

2. They created a pamphlet with Styrofoam pros and cons and passed it out.

3. They polled the student body to see if people would pay an extra nickel for paper trays; 85% of students said they would.

4. They sent the poll results to the school board.

5. The board agreed to make both paper and Styrofoam trays available for a week—to see if kids would *really* choose paper.

6. Tanja remembers, "A lot of kids got so enthusiastic—they were giving out nickels so kids who forgot extra money could buy paper trays." By the end of the week, 86% of the students had paid the extra nickel.

7. When the school board heard the results, the members voted unanimously to use paper trays.

Achievements

Tanja and other West Milford H.S. students went to the United Nations to participate in the Youth Environmental Forum. They shared their story with kids from all over the world.

YOU CAN BE A HERO

Help promote alternatives to Styrofoam. For more information:

• You can write to Tanja at 70 Mountain Circle, West Milford, NJ 07480. Tell her what kind of information you want and include a self-addressed, stamped, 11" x 17" envelope with $2.00 in postage on it.

• **Local Solutions to Global Pollution**, 2121 Bonar St., Berkeley, CA 94702. Ask for an order form that shows what information you can get. Send a self-addressed, stamped envelope.

JUST SAY YES

Group: Youth for Environmental Sanity (YES!)

Ages: 17-19   **Town:** Santa Cruz, California

Goal: "Educate, inspire, and empower students to take positive action for our planet and our future"

WHAT THEY DID

Summary

In 1990, 16-year-old Ocean Robbins noticed that many of his friends and acquaintances had a hopeless feeling about the environment and the future. "They didn't think they could do anything about these massive problems," he says.

But he and Ryan Eliason don't believe young people are powerless. "The question isn't, 'Do I make a difference?' says Ryan. "It's 'Do I want to make a *positive* difference or a *negative* one?'"

The result: They started the YES! tour to visit U.S. schools, speaking to kids and motivating them to help solve environmental problems. "But it isn't just an inspiring message," says Ocean, "We try to get people to take personal responsibility for improving the future of life on Earth."

Results

They have visited schools in 15 states, inspiring thousands of students to form eco-clubs (to get their schools to buy recycled paper products, recycle, etc.). Some 7-10-year-olds in Portland, Oregon, were so enthusiastic that they formed their own, younger version of the YES! tour, called Youth for Environmental Awareness (YEA!).

HOW THEY DID IT

1. They gathered a group of local high-school kids who wanted to participate in the group. There were 6 people the first year.

2. They specified that the group be entirely student-run.

3. They came up with a presentation. They included:

• A game show skit called "We're in Jeopardy," in which the contestants (stereotypical high schoolers, like a nerd and a cheerleader) are asked questions on the environment.

• Talks about why they're on the tour. For example, group member Sol Solomon explains how he's afraid concern for the environment is being treated like a fad...then he suggests ways to keep it from becoming one.

• A slide show on how the Earth is being destroyed, and how people are taking action to stop it.

• Audience participation. For example, the group members shout out questions like "Can we make a difference?" and everyone answers "Yes!"

4. They planned to perform the show in each area for a week, then hold an all-day workshop for interested kids. "Public speaking is inspiring, but workshops are where we really felt we could empower people and train them to be effective activists," says Ryan.

5. They called TV stations and newspapers to get publicity.

They appeared on TV in *The Home Show*. Newspapers like *USA Today* printed stories about them.

6. Students from schools all over the country called to invite them to their campuses.

7. They had to raise money to go on tour. Schools were asked to pay $150 for appearances, and YES! members contacted companies, foundations and individuals to ask for donations.

8. The YES! group went on tour. Ocean notes: "We didn't just go to environmentally aware places like California; we included places like Arkansas, Texas, Oklahoma, Kansas, Missouri— and inner city areas."

YOU CAN BE A HERO

Want to have YES! come to your school?
• For information, contact the group members at 706 Frederick St., Santa Cruz, CA 95062.

Another option: Start your own "eco-tour" to local schools.
• For ideas on how to get started, contact YES! (address above). They'll send a "Student Action Guide" for $3.95 that tells how to form a club, have successful meetings, etc. raise money.

OUT OF
THE OZONE

Name: Russell Essary
Age: 7   **Grade:** 2
Town: Forest Hills,
New York
School: P.S. 174Q
Goal: Help keep the
ozone layer from disap-
pearing by keeping
chlorofluorocarbons
(CFCs) out of the air

WHAT HE DID

Summary

One hot day in 1989, Russell and his father, Gayle, were
driving to his grandmother's house without the car air condi-
tioning on. Russell asked why. His father said it would dam-
age the ozone layer—the invisible shield around the Earth
that protects us from harmful sunlight. How? The coolant
used in car air conditioners is made of chemicals called chlorofluorocarbons (CFCs) that evaporate and "eat" the ozone.

That night, Russell felt sad. He started crying because he
felt so hopeless about the ozone problem. His mother told his
father that "little kids shouldn't be worried about things un-
less they can do something about them." His dad agreed, saying, "Even a child like you *can* do something if you take the
time and the energy and stick with it."

Encouraged by this advice, Russell started a group called

KiDS STOP (Kids Save the Ozone Project).

Results

Russell's campaign helped persuade lawmakers to phase out all CFCs in America and require the U.S. to help other countries stop using them, too.

HOW HE DID IT

1. Russell, his sister, Melanie, and their father sent away for information about the depletion of the ozone layer so they could explain the problem when people asked questions.

2. Russell asked kids at school to join his group. Nine were interested right away; eventually 23 children joined.

3. Their city councilman, Sheldon Leffler, heard about what they were doing. He had the kids come to city hall to "testify"—talk about the problems CFCs are causing for the Earth. Then he introduced a New York City bill that would require car air conditioner fluid to be recycled. (CFCs escape when they're not recycled.)

4. The KiDS STOP campaign was publicized in newspapers and on TV, and people started writing to Russell from all over the country.

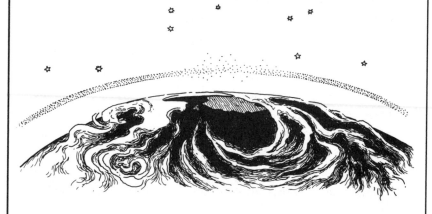

5. They made information packets with tips for people who wanted to start "No CFC" campaigns in their areas.

6. The CFC recycling bill passed....But the mayor of New York City vetoed it (turned it down).

7. When a new mayor was elected, the kids lobbied him to support a state bill like the one that had been vetoed. This one passed and became a law.

8. More progress: Environmental groups like the Natural Resources Defense Council had also been working on getting CFCs phased out. And one senator, Albert Gore, convinced Congress to ban CFCs as part of the Clean Air Act.

9. There was one more obstacle—other countries could still use CFCs. But the U.S. government wouldn't help pay to get them to stop.

10. KiDS STOP was invited to an event called the United Nations' Environmental Youth Forum. While the kids were there, they passed out fliers asking the director of the program to contact President Bush and ask him to support a worldwide ban on CFCs. The director agreed with the kids. He called the Prime Minister of England, who called President Bush. It worked; Bush supported the effort.

Achievements
Russell won the President's Environmental Youth Award.

YOU CAN BE A HERO
Find out about upcoming KiDS STOP (Now called "KiDS Save The Planet") projects.

• Write to the group at P.O. Box 471, Forest Hills, NY 11375. If you include a self-addressed, stamped envelope with $2 in postage on it, they'll send you a free information packet that tells how you can start and run a project.

THE ENVIRONMENT SHOW

Group: Peace Child Repertory Theatre   **Ages:** 11-22
Town: Los Angeles, California
Goal: Raise people's awareness about the environment by performing theatrical productions

WHAT THEY DID

Summary

In 1988, a group of kids in Los Angeles started a repertory theatre to address issues that are important to children.

Environmental issues were top priority for all the members of the group, so they created "The Environment Show." It's now one of their most popular productions.

The 30-minute play is designed to make people think about the Earth; it's filled with facts about problems like the disappearing ozone layer and the garbage crisis. The cast does skits about people who are damaging the earth. "We're very direct—we don't beat around the bush," says cast member Erika Goodkin.

Results

The play's message has reached thousands of people at performances in California, Arizona, Colorado, and New Mexico. Erika says the performance scares people because they haven't realized how serious environmental issues are, or how much kids know about them. "At the end, they're sitting there with their mouths open, crying...It blows their minds," she says.

HOW THEY DID IT

1. They did research on environmental issues. "We had everyone assigned to a topic, like Styrofoam or the rainforests," says cast member Julia Parmenter.

2. Skits started as informal "improvisations." For example: Two people played a military general and a child discussing pollution.

3. Other cast members commented on the dialogue, pointing out when it wasn't realistic and suggesting improvements.

4. They wrote the final versions of each skit. Then someone typed and copied them.

5. They revised the skits and added songs.

6. They decided who would be best to play each part.

7. The cast rehearsed the show in 4-hour sessions.

8. They performed in different outfits, depending on where they were. Their standard costume: Colorful beach pants and T-shirts, to symbolize that people are all different.

9. Every now and then, they update the script according to current events. For example, after the Persian Gulf War they added a skit about oil fires in Kuwait.

YOU CAN BE A HERO

Gather your classmates, youth group members—even your brothers and sisters—and create a play about the environment:

• Include facts about the Earth. For example: "Every minute, an area of rainforest the size of a football field is destroyed." Where do you find them? Books like *50 Simple Things Kids Can Do to Save the Earth*, encyclopedias (recent ones), magazines like *National Geographic* and newspapers.

• How to think up skits: Janet Parmenter, the group's co-advisor,

says, "Listen to the way people talk to each other and use it as the basis of your dialogue—the play could simply be 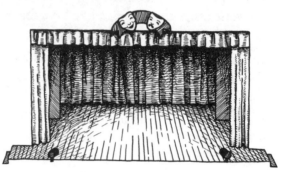 about a bunch of kids talking." You can also do a complete story rather than a series of skits.

• At some point, tell the audience what they can do to solve the environmental problems you're discussing.

• Where should you perform? Start with a show at someone's house (for friends, parents, and neighbors). If your group wants to continue, see if schools or churches are interested in hosting a show.

For Peace Child Repertory Theatre performance information:
• Send a self-addressed, stamped envelope to Peace Child Repertory Theatre, P.O. BOX 224, Agoura Hills, CA 91301.

A GOOD SIGN

Name: Melissa Poe

Age: 11   **Grade:** 6

Town: Nashville, Tennessee

Goal: Encourage world leaders (and other people) to help stop pollution

WHAT SHE DID

Summary

When Melissa was 9, she saw an episode of a TV program called *Highway to Heaven* that showed how polluted the world might become. She says, "I was scared I might die young because of it—that the world would be an ugly place to live, and my kids might die young."

She wrote to President Bush, asking him to help stop pollution, but he never wrote back. She didn't want him to ignore her letter "just because it was from a kid." So she came up with another way to get his attention: She called an advertising billboard company and asked them to put her letter on a board.

Results

Her letter ended up on a billboard in Washington, D.C... and in many other U.S. cities. The President *still* didn't write (he only sent a form letter about drug abuse), but kids interested in stopping pollution did. So Melissa started a club called Kids For A Clean Environment (Kids FACE). It now has 30,000 members and chapters all over the world.

HOW SHE DID IT

1. She wrote the letter:

Dear Mr. President,

"I want to keep on living till I am 100 years old. Right now I am 9 years old. My name is Melissa. You and other people, maybe you could put up signs saying: Stop Pollution, It's Killing the World. PLEASE help me stop pollution Mr. President. Please, if you ignore this letter, soon we will die of pollution of the ozone layer."

Please help,

Melissa

2. When she got no response, she decided to make her own signs with markers, and put them up herself.

3. Her mother suggested she call a billboard company and ask them to do the signs instead; that way, they would be bigger and more people would see them.

4. Melissa looked in the phone book under billboard companies. "I just picked one," she says.

5. She called and told a woman named Karen she wanted to put up a billboard in Nashville for free.

6. Karen asked if it was for a nonprofit organization, and Melissa said "I guess so." It was free, but she had to pay for the paper—which cost $50—and fill out a form.

7. Melissa had a yard sale the next day to raise the money.

8. She received the form, filled it out, and sent it back. Karen brought it to her manager, who decided Melissa

wouldn't have to pay the $50 after all, because what she was doing was "too important." They even decided to help Melissa get more billboards.

9. Melissa asked if they could get one in Washington. They said they couldn't, but referred her to a Washington company that was happy to help out.

YOU CAN BE A HERO
Speak up: Write letters about the environment to your city's mayor or a local newspaper editor. Some hints:

• Melissa has found it helps to write about the future. She recommends: "Put something in like, 'In 20 years, I'll be 30, and I don't want to live with so much pollution.' That makes people think." Then ask for their help.

• Write your letters by hand. Handwritten notes from children get special treatment in many government offices. "If you type, they don't know you're a kid," says Melissa.

• Encourage your parents and friends to write letters.

• To join Kids FACE (it's free) or start a chapter, write to P.O. Box 158254, Nashville, Tennessee 37215. You'll get a book, membership certificate, and newsletter.

A BURNING ISSUE

Name: Kory Johnson
Age: 12   **Grade:** 6
Town: Phoenix, Arizona
School: Peralta Elementary School
Goal: Stop an incinerator from burning hazardous waste near her town.

WHAT SHE DID
Summary
Kory's sister died because her mother drank contaminated well water while she was pregnant.

As a result, Kory decided to take a stand against pollution. She started a group called Children for a Safe Environment; now she and her mother are two of Arizona's most respected environmental activists.

Their latest accomplishment: Leading a protest against a company which was about to start burning hazardous waste—70% of it from out of state.

The Johnsons' job wasn't easy because the Arizona state government had made a deal with the company. The struggle lasted a year and a half, and their house became a temporary Greenpeace headquarters and "hotel" for people helping with the protest.

Results
There was so much public pressure against the incinerator that on May 5, 1991, the governor of Arizona informed

company officials that the deal was off. He later admitted, "If I hadn't done that, my kids wouldn't have let me come home tonight!"

HOW SHE DID IT

1. Kory wrote letters protesting the incinerator to the governor, local newspaper, health department, and department of environmental quality.

2. She mailed letters and fliers about the issue to local residents. Kory and her mother were so busy that even on Thanksgiving, they were folding and addressing 2,500 fliers. "The turkey tasted like stamps," says her mother.

3. Kory spoke to the press at the incinerator site.

4. She helped organize and stage a protest at the state capitol. Kory and other people sat in a bed wearing Groucho Marx glasses and exchanging fake money, with a

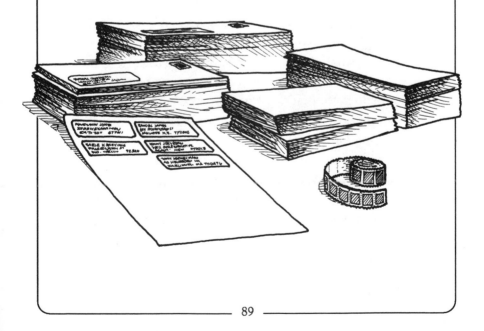

sign that said: "Why are government agencies in bed with toxic polluters?"

5. A candlelight rally was held at the capitol. For 3 hours, children from all over the state, including a Native American Indian reservation in Northern Arizona, went up to the microphone and spoke about protecting the environment.

6. During the rally, kids' anti-incinerator artwork was on display inside the capitol.

Achievements

Kory is the first person to receive John Denver's Windstar Environmental Youth Award. She was also chosen as a "Giraffe" by the Giraffe Project, which honors activists for their work.

YOU CAN BE A HERO

Get involved in a community action project.

• Kory says, "Saving cans and newspapers is great, but there are so many other environment-related things you can do."

• Find out what's happening in your area. How? Read the newspaper. You might find an article about a proposed landfill or incinerator that many people oppose.

• Does the article mention an environmental group working on the issue? If it does, call the organization and volunteer to help. These groups usually welcome kids' participation.

• If you don't find any projects, call local groups like the Sierra Club or Audubon Society and ask what campaigns they're involved with. (Groups are listed under "Environmental" in the yellow pages.)

KIDS' ECO-GROUPS

*Want to get more involved? Contact some of these groups.
They'll send you information about what they're
doing. They might direct you to local groups
in your area...or maybe even invite you to travel around
and talk to other kids about the environment.*

• **Earth Train,** 900 N. Point, San Francisco, CA 94109.
A group of 200 children who will begin touring the U.S.,
Europe and Japan giving seminars on the environment in
1992. Write to them for information about becoming a
participant.

• **Environmental Youth Alliance,** P.O. Box 34097, Station
D, Vancouver, B.C. V6J 4M1, Canada. Works on different
issues, including the protection of old growth forests. For
information, send a self-addressed envelope with $1.50
postage on it.

• **Caretakers of the Environment International/USA,** 2216
Schiller Ave., Wilmette, IL 60091. Helps high school
students reach others who want to get involved with
environment-related projects. They offer free guidelines for
organizing a group.

• **Children for Old Growth,** P.O. Box 1090, Redway, CA
95560. Membership costs $10. Dedicated to saving our
ancient forests. If you join, you'll get a large poster of a forest
and receive newsletters written by kids.

• **Children's Alliance for Protection of the Environment (CAPE),** P.O. Box 307, Austin, TX 78767. An international organization with information about kids' projects and how you can join them. Has a newspaper written by children called "Many Hands"—ask for a free copy.

• **Ground Truth Studies Project,** The Aspen Global Change Institute, 100 East Francis, Aspen, CO 81611. An educational program that helps children understand that events in their local environment are related to global environmental change.

• **Kids Against Pollution (KAP),** Tenakill School, P.O. Box 775, Closter, NJ 07624. Started by elementary school students, this group is now for kids of all ages. For $6, you can become a member, get a packet of info about stopping pollution, and find out what other kids in KAP are doing.

• **Kids For A Clean Environment (Kids FACE),** P.O. Box 158254, Nashville, TN 37215. Melissa Poe's group (see p. 86). Membership is free; you'll get a newsletter and other interesting materials.

• **Kids for Saving the Earth (KSE),** P.O. Box 47247, Plymouth, MN 55447. They'll send you an information packet to help you start your own environmental club. Sponsored by Target Stores.

• **Kids Network,** National Geographic Society, Educational Services, Dept. 1001, Washington, D.C. 20077. (800) 368-2728. Has computerized classes that allow students to communicate with other students about topics like acid rain and water pollution. Have your teacher call for details.

• **KiDS STOP (Kids Save the Planet!)** P.O. Box 471, Forest Hills, NY 11375. Originally called Kids Save The Ozone Project (see p. 79), this group is now working on other issues. For info, send a self-addressed stamped envelope with $2 worth of postage on it.

• **People Educating Other People for a Long-Lasting Environment (Project PEOPLE),** P.O. Box 932, Prospect Heights, IL 60070. Run by elementary school students; you can receive their newsletter for $5 a year.

• **Student Conservation Association,** 1800 N. Kent St., Suite 1260, Arlington, VA 22209. Helps high school students get summer jobs in parks; offers field experience programs. Their newsletter costs $16.95 for 6 issues.

• **Student Environmental Action Coalition (SEAC),** P.O. Box 1168, Chapel Hill, NC 27514-1168. A national support group for high school (and college) activists.

• **Youth for Environmental Sanity (YES!),** 706 Frederick St., Santa Cruz, CA 95062. A student group that visits schools to talk about the environment (see p. 76 for their story). They also have a student action guide.

GROUPS HONORING KID HEROES

*If you're doing something to help save the environment,
you may be selected by some of these groups to be recognized
or win an award—if they know about you.
Write or call them for an application and details.*

• **Environmental Exchange,** 1930 18th St. NW, Suite 24, Washington, D.C. 20009. They tell the media about people who are helping protect the environment. Write to them for details.

• **Giraffe Project,** P.O. Box 759, Langley, WA 98260. (800) 344-TALL. "Giraffes" are kids and adults who take a risk—"stick their necks out"—to help the environment or other causes. It's best if someone else (like a teacher or community leader) nominates you.

• **Keep America Beautiful National Awards Program,** Mill River Plaza, 9 West Broad St., Stamford, CT 06902. Has a youth awards category. The deadline for entering is in August. Call for an application.

• **Kids for Saving the Earth (KSE),** P.O. Box 47247, Plymouth, MN 55447. Recognizes kids' environmental clubs and groups. Write for more information.

• **President's Environmental Youth Awards,** 401 M St. SW, Washington, D.C. 20460. July 31 is the deadline; to apply, you need to be 18 or under and have an adult sponsor. Write for an application. Note: Your science teacher or youth group leader may have an application, too.

• **Searching for Success,** Renew America, 1400 Sixteenth St. NW, Suite 710, Washington, D.C. 20036. Award categories include energy efficiency, wildlife conservation, solid waste reduction, and others. The deadline is January 15.

• **United Nations Environment Programme,** Dulcie de Montagnac, Room DC 1-590, United Nations, New York, NY 10017. (212) 963-4931. Not an awards program but a summer "forum," where kids from all over the world talk about the projects they're doing. Call for an application.

• **Windstar Youth Award,** 2317 Snowmass Creek Rd., Snowmass, CO 81654. John Denver gives this scholarship award to kids. Write for an application—nominations are due by April 1.

ARE YOU A HERO?

If you're doing something to help save the Earth, to help other people, to make your town a better place to live—or anything you're really proud of—we'd like to hear about it. Please make a copy of this form, fill it out, and mail it to:

Kid Heroes
EarthWorks Press
1400 Shattuck Ave. #25
Berkeley, CA 94709

Name_____

Age_____ Grade_____ School_____

Address_____

_____

Telephone number (_____)_____

What you or your group did:

_____

_____

_____

_____

_____

_____

_____

_____

_____

_____